SHOCK ZONE™
TRUE SURVIVAL STORIES

SuRVIVING
in COLD PLACES

CARLA MOONEY

Lerner Publications Company • Minneapolis

Lerner Publications Company
A division of Lerner Publishing Group, Inc.
241 First Avenue North
Minneapolis, MN 55401 U.S.A.

For reading levels and more information, look up this title at
www.lernerbooks.com.

Library of Congress Cataloging-in-Publication Data

Mooney, Carla, 1970–
     Surviving in cold places / by Carla Mooney.
         pages   cm. — (Shockzone—True survival stories)
     Includes index.
     ISBN 978–1–4677–1434–1 (lib. bdg. : alk. paper)
     ISBN 978–1–4677–2514–9 (eBook)
     1. Survival—Polar regions—Juvenile literature. 2. Polar regions—Environmental
   conditions—Juvenile literature. I. Title.
   GF86.M66 2014
   363.34092'211—dc23   2013019868

Manufactured in the United States of America
1 — PC — 12/31/13

TABLE OF CONTENTS

INTO THE DEEP FREEZE

Have you ever wondered what you would do if you were stranded in the cold and snow? We're not talking about just staying outside too long in your backyard in the winter. Imagine being far from shelter in temperatures so cold your fingers and toes freeze solid. Blizzards so intense you can't see your hand in front of your face. Surrounded by snowdrifts so deep you have to struggle for each step. Would you have the guts to make hard choices?

Could you survive?

Here are six stories of people who answered yes. They survived the coldest, harshest environments on the planet and lived to tell the tales. None of them expected to face a fight for their lives when they set out. For some, the cold took their fingers, their toes, or even their friends' lives. Yet, when faced with a life-or-death struggle, each survivor found the courage to keep going. Through ice, snow, and bitter cold, they found a way to make it out alive.

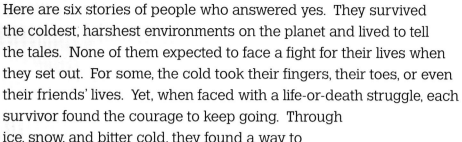

Surviving in frigid temperatures takes special determination. Do you think you've got what it takes?

On Christmas Day 1943, First Lieutenant Leon Crane took off into the cold Alaska air in his B-24 bomber. The copilot and his four crew members were scheduled for a routine test flight. But about 120 miles (193 kilometers) east of Fairbanks, the plane went into a violent spin. Unable to control the aircraft, Crane knew there was only one option left. Bail out! Crane and two of his men managed to strap on their parachutes and escape into the frigid air. The other two men were unable to grab their parachutes in time and went down with the plane.

The pilot drifted down through the air, eventually landing in hip-deep snow on a steep mountainside. He yelled for the other survivors but heard only the echo of his own voice. Looking up, he spotted the plane's burning wreckage farther up the mountain. Crane knew from his training that he should stay with the wrecked airplane so that rescuers could find him. But the mountain's slope

Crane feared that a rescue team would not be able to find him before he starved or froze to death. If he were to survive, he would have to take action on his own. He took stock of his supplies. Besides his flight suit, he had a few matches, a knife, and the parachute he landed with. There was no food to be found. Even worse, Crane had lost his gloves in the bailout. His hands were in danger of freezing in the subzero temperatures—another reason for him to get moving.

Crane trudged slowly through the snow until he reached a river. He figured that if anyone lived in the area, it would be near the water. As night fell, he gathered tree branches and lit a fire with his matches. Then he wrapped himself in his parachute and tried to sleep. With no food or gloves, his chances of survival were slim.

Wintertime in Alaska can be as deadly as it is beautiful.

As the days passed at the stream, there was no sign of other people. Crane's hands were numb and bleeding, and without food, he was quickly losing strength. Finally, he decided he had to move again, so he started hiking downriver. After a few torturous days, Crane stumbled upon a tiny cabin. In parts of Alaska, it is a tradition for people with cabins to leave them unlocked with supplies inside for travelers in need. In the cabin, Crane found food, a stove, wood, warm clothing, and a rifle. He thought he might be near rescuers. But in reality, the closest town was 100 miles (160 km) away.

For six weeks, Crane stayed in the cabin. He ate only tiny amounts of the food to make it last as long as possible, and he rested to regain his strength. When the food ran low, Crane left the cabin and headed

Finding an unlocked cabin filled with supplies gave Crane a chance to survive.

downriver again. At one point, he fell into the icy waters. His wet clothes quickly froze, so he built a fire to dry himself out. After two weeks of traveling, Crane found another stocked cabin. He stayed there for several days before continuing along the river. Eight long days later, he spotted a recently used sled dog trail. He followed it to yet another cabin. But this time, he could hear dogs barking and children playing. For the first time in weeks, Crane saw fellow human beings.

Inside the cabin, a trapper and his family listened to Crane's incredible story. It had been more than eighty days since his B-24 went down, and he had walked a total of 120 miles (193 km) along the river. The trapper gave Crane a ride on his dogsled to the nearest town. There, a plane took Crane back to his air base. His fellow pilots were stunned to learn he was alive. Incredibly, he had not lost a significant amount of weight during his ordeal. Against the odds, the airman had survived alone in one of the world's harshest climates. His fellow crewmen who parachuted out of the plane were not so lucky. They were never seen alive again. The body of one, Second Lieutenant Harold Hoskin, was recovered in 2006.

When he returned to base, Crane (*lower right*) told his story to his amazed fellow airmen.

Defying Death in Antarctica

At the bottom of the world, Australian explorer Douglas Mawson prepared to explore uncharted land. It would be the most dangerous exploration of his life.

In 1912 Mawson led the Australasian Antarctic Expedition. The thirty-one men on the expedition built a camp on an Antarctic cove called Commonwealth Bay. This perilous area is widely known as one of the windiest places on Earth. Gusts can top 150 miles (240 km) per hour. In November the men split into teams of three. Each team journeyed into different parts of Antarctica for scientific work.

Mawson chose the most dangerous path. His team, the Far Eastern Party, would explore several glaciers and travel hundreds of miles from camp. The two men traveling with Mawson were Belgrave Ninnis, a British army officer, and Xavier Mertz, a Swiss champion skier. They loaded three sleds with food, survival gear, and other supplies. They harnessed sixteen husky dogs to pull the sled.

Then they set off into the frozen unknown. On the journey, they crossed two major glaciers. They safely traveled over many hidden crevasses.

By day 35, Mawson's team had traveled almost 300 miles (480 km) from camp. Mertz signaled to warn the team about another crevasse, and Mawson carefully guided his sled over it. But when he looked back, Ninnis and his sled had vanished. He had fallen through the snow-covered crevasse and was lost in the abyss. Also lost were the team's tent, six huskies, and most of their food. Looking into the crevasse, Mawson and Mertz saw some of the supplies and dogs on a distant ledge. But Ninnis was never seen again.

Mawson and Mertz were unable to see their companion in the deep, dark crevasse.

Eating his sled dogs after they collapsed may have led to Mertz's death.

With little food, the two men knew they would have to turn back right away. One by one, the remaining dogs collapsed during the frantic return journey. The men shot the fallen dogs and ate their meat. As they pushed toward camp, Mertz became ill. By January 7, his condition had worsened. He talked nonsense and tried to rip their shelter apart. Mawson tried to calm Mertz and tucked him into a sleeping bag. Overnight, the Swiss skier died in his sleep. Years later, researchers suspected Mertz may have gotten vitamin A poisoning from eating the livers of the fallen dogs. He did not like the tougher muscle meat, so he ate more of the livers than Mawson did.

Weak and alone, Mawson pushed ahead. His food was almost gone. He still had 100 miles (160 km) to travel to reach camp. Suddenly, Mawson felt the snow give way beneath him. He had fallen into a crevasse. He dangled from his harness as his sled caught on the sides of the crack in the ice. Miraculously, the sled held. Slowly and painfully, Mawson pulled himself up the harness rope. He dragged his sled from the crevasse and continued moving.

Finally, on February 8, Mawson could see Commonwealth Bay. In the distance, he spotted the *Aurora*, the ship that had brought the group to Antarctica. It was leaving the bay for good. Mawson was afraid he had missed his chance for rescue. But as he approached the camp, he saw a few men. They had remained behind to look for Mawson and his team. He finally reached Australia in February of the next year. The country greeted this incredible survivor as a national hero.

COLD WEATHER CLOTHING

Want to keep warm in the cold? Try dressing in several layers of loose-fitting, lightweight, warm clothing. The layers will trap air between them, which keeps your body warm. Over the layers, a water-repellent, tightly woven coat or similar item will keep the wet out and the heat in. Be sure to put on a hat, since much of your body heat escapes through your head. To protect your lungs from the cold, use a scarf or other material to cover your mouth.

Missing the departure of the *Aurora* by just five hours extended Mawson's expedition by nearly a year.

MIRACLE ON MAMMOTH MOUNTAIN

Eric LeMarque always liked the cold and ice. He was not only a former professional hockey player but also an expert skier and snowboarder. In early 2004, Eric had no idea his next adventure would nearly be his last.

On February 6, Eric prepared for one last run down California's Mammoth Mountain. He had spent the past week skiing and snowboarding down the 11,000-foot (3,350-meter) peak with friends. When his friends left that morning, Eric decided to stay to get in a few more runs down the mountain. Figuring he would just be out for a few hours, Eric wore a light jacket, a long-sleeve shirt, a

Eric made several long runs near the mountain's southern end. For his last run, Eric spotted a path of fresh snow in an area called Dragon's Back. There is no chairlift in that area. People who snowboard down Dragon's Back have to climb up the mountain. But that didn't stop Eric. After climbing up the mountain and snowboarding back down, Eric came to a flat area. He decided to walk back to the resort. But fog made it difficult to see, and he went the wrong way. He headed into the wilderness. It was late afternoon. It was getting dark.

When night fell on Mammoth Mountain, Eric's chances of survival began to look slim.

Unable to signal for help from the air, Eric knew he would have to rely on himself to survive even longer.

As night fell, the temperature dropped into the single digits. Eric realized that he was lost. All he had in his pockets were four pieces of gum, an MP3 player, a wet bag of matches, and a cell phone with a dead battery. He tried to build a fire, but the wet matches would not light. Nervous and cold, he dug a trench in the snow to get out of the whipping winter winds and tried to sleep.

The next day, Eric decided to hike in a direction he hoped would bring him to the nearby Tamarack Lodge resort. He never found it. Instead, he hiked farther into the wilderness. To survive, he ate bark and pine nuts. He slept in snow trenches to protect himself from the bitter winds. Eric tried to use the blue screen of his MP3 player to signal airplanes or helicopters, but the screen was too small to be seen from the air.

Using his MP3 player, Eric discovered a radio signal. When he faced the player in a certain direction, the signal got stronger. He realized then that he had been hiking away from the nearest village. Over the next few days, Eric grew weaker. He struggled to walk back the way he had come. His feet bled and turned black from frostbite. After seven days in the wilderness, Eric was completely exhausted. Meanwhile, Eric's parents were frantic with worry. No one had spoken to him since he'd parted ways with his friends seven days earlier. Rescuers believed that no one could have survived the freezing temperatures without shelter for that long. They sent a helicopter to look for Eric's body.

Eric was unable to walk. He lay down in the snow. Suddenly, he heard a helicopter. Help had finally arrived. However, Eric's ordeal was not over. He had suffered through extreme cold and was badly dehydrated. In the hospital, doctors amputated Eric's legs 6 inches (15 centimeters) below the knee. He was fitted with artificial legs and feet. Eric refused to let this setback stop him. Over several months, he learned how to walk on prosthetic legs. He even returned to snowboarding!

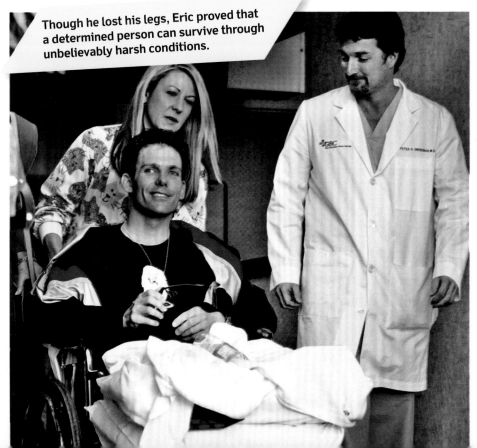

Though he lost his legs, Eric proved that a determined person can survive through unbelievably harsh conditions.

Snowbound in Nevada

For Californians Jim and Jennifer Stolpa, a drive to a family funeral quickly turned into a snowbound nightmare. In December 1992, Jim's grandmother died. On December 29, the couple and their five-month-old baby boy, Clayton, climbed into a pickup truck. They headed over the Sierra Nevada for the funeral in Idaho.

Meanwhile, a fierce snowstorm battered the region. Several roads were closed, including Interstate 80, the highway they planned to take. Jim and Jennifer decided to take a remote route. As they drove, the snow continued to fall heavily. It grew deeper and deeper, until finally the truck became stuck. For four days, the couple and their baby huddled in the truck, hoping for someone to drive by. They ate corn chips, coconut cookies, fruitcakes, and Jennifer's vitamins. No one came. No one even knew where the Stolpas were.

On January 2, Jim and Jennifer decided they had to find help. They put on every piece of clothing they had. They slipped plastic garbage bags between layers of socks. They wore sweatshirts on their heads. They bundled Clayton inside a garment bag and pulled it through the snow like a sled. The family trekked through the night. But they could not find the highway. They huddled beneath overhanging rocks. In the morning, the snow began to fall again. Jennifer told Jim she couldn't walk anymore. So they found a small cave. Jennifer crawled inside with the baby. Jim tucked them in with a sleeping bag. Then he told Jennifer that he was going to find help.

That night, Jim walked 14 miles (23 km) in the snow back to the truck. Early the next morning, he hiked again, pushing through deep snow. When he felt hungry, he ate snow. Late on the morning of January 6, Jim spotted a pickup truck coming down the road. When Jim told the driver about Jennifer and the baby, the driver quickly organized a rescue effort. Jim wanted to join the rescuers, but his feet were frozen solid. He told the rescuers where to look for his family. For five hours, the rescuers searched for Jennifer and the baby. It was almost nighttime, and snow was beginning to fall again. The rescuers began to lose hope of finding the stranded mother and child. Then one of the rescuers radioed that he had found them. Jennifer immediately asked about Jim. The rescuers reassured her that he was alive. Both Jim and Jennifer had severe frostbite. Amazingly, baby Clayton survived the ordeal with only a case of diaper rash.

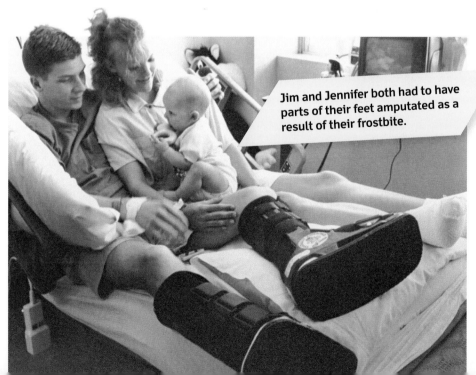

Jim and Jennifer both had to have parts of their feet amputated as a result of their frostbite.

THE INCREDIBLE VOYAGE OF THE ENDURANCE

In August 1914, Irish explorer Sir Ernest Shackleton set out on a dangerous expedition. He planned to make the first crossing of Earth's deadliest continent: Antarctica. Shackleton's ship *Endurance* stopped in Buenos Aires, Argentina, and then at a whaling station on South Georgia Island before setting out for Antarctica in December 1914. Although Shackleton commanded the ship, it also had a captain, Frank Worsley.

Explorers had visited Antarctica before, but no one had ever crossed the entire continent. The crew would attempt the journey on dogsleds. A second ship would pick them up on the other side. They didn't have much time. Seasons in the Southern Hemisphere are opposite of those in the Northern Hemisphere. After March, the Antarctic winter would arrive. Antarctic winters bring incredibly cold conditions. And in the southernmost parts of the continent, it remains dark twenty-four hours a day for the entire six-month winter

For six weeks, the ship dodged and rammed through huge, floating blocks of ice in the Southern Ocean. By January 18, 1915, the *Endurance* was just one day from the planned landing point in Antarctica. But the freezing weather would rip those plans to shreds. That night, ice closed around the ship like concrete, stopping it cold. With winter approaching, Shackleton and his men were stranded in the coldest climate on Earth.

Shackleton prepared his men to tough out the winter aboard the frozen ship. For ten months, the ship drifted with the ice for hundreds of miles. The crew watched nervously as ice pressed on the ship. The *Endurance*'s wood timbers began to crack and groan. Eventually, the pressure crushed the ship beyond repair. The crew was forced into lifeboats. They moved onto the ice and set up a camp. When their supply of food ran out, the men hunted penguins and seals. They even shot and ate their sled dogs. As each day passed, their ice camp continued to drift in the Antarctic waters. As 1916 arrived, the men waited helplessly on the moving ice.

Destroyed by ice, the *Endurance* finally sank on November 21, 1915.

The six men packed into the tiny lifeboat knew that the lives of the entire crew were in their hands.

In April 1916, the ice grew thin. On April 9, the crew boarded the three remaining lifeboats. They set a course for uninhabited Elephant Island, about 100 miles (160 km) to the north. Rough seas threatened the men's lives. But on the seventh day of the journey, the boats landed at Elephant Island.

The men were not out of trouble yet. Elephant Island is extremely remote, and Shackleton doubted rescuers would find them there. He knew another treacherous voyage in the lifeboats would be necessary. He chose five of his toughest sailors and asked them to join him on the 800-mile (1,300 km) crossing to the islands of South Georgia. On April 24, Shackleton and the five men set sail. Worsley plotted the course. If his navigational measurements were off, the men would be stranded at sea, hundreds of miles from the nearest human being.

Meanwhile, the rest of the crew waited on Elephant Island. Many suffered from frostbite or illness. Their scarce shelter and threadbare clothing did little to comfort them in the extreme cold. They overturned the two remaining lifeboats to create huts, and they used seal blubber to power lamps. To gather food, they organized daily hunting expeditions. And they kept watch for Shackleton's return.

On May 10, Shackleton's boat landed on South Georgia. But it had landed on the wrong side of the island. Ships and rescuers were on the opposite side. Ten days later, after a difficult hike, Shackleton and the men walked into a whaling station. Immediately, Shackleton made a plan to rescue the crew members left on Elephant Island. Over the next few months, Shackleton tried several times to send a rescue team. Each time, ice or rough weather forced the rescuers to turn back. Finally, four months after he left on the lifeboat, Shackleton finally reached his men. Against all odds, he had saved every one.

THE EFFECTS OF FROSTBITE

When exposed to very cold temperatures, your skin and tissues can freeze, resulting in frostbite. Your hands, feet, nose, and ears are most likely to be affected by frostbite. Skin that looks white or grayish yellow and is very cold or hard may have frostbite. Severe frostbite can cause blisters, hardening, and the loss of feeling. If you think you have frostbite, you should seek medical help right away. A medical professional can help you gradually warm the affected area.

The crew of the *Endurance* stayed alive by creating ingenious shelters and searching for food.

Alive in the Andes

Did you ever imagine a routine airplane flight could turn into a nightmarish struggle for survival? On October 13, 1972, an airplane carrying forty-five people flew over the Andes Mountains in Argentina. Many of the passengers were members of a rugby team from Uruguay. They were flying to Chile for a rugby match. They never made it.

In the middle of the flight, the plane slammed into a mountain peak, snapping off its wings and tail. The main body of the plane slid down the snow-covered slope like an out-of-control sled. Finally, the plane stopped abruptly. Many seats broke loose from the floor, and passengers were thrown forward. Some were crushed by the impact.

Twenty-seven passengers survived the crash. Many were badly injured. Most were wearing only summer clothes. They had no blankets or warm coats to protect them against the bitter cold of the high mountain peaks. At night the temperature dropped to −30°F (−34°C). To keep warm, the passengers used the thin seat covers for blankets.

For the first few days after the crash, the passengers believed that a rescue party would find them. While they waited, Marcelo Perez, the rugby team captain, took charge. He organized the passengers to clear debris from the plane, melt snow into water, and huddle closely together to keep warm. But after ten days, no rescue had arrived. Listening to a small transistor radio, the passengers heard that the search for them had been called off. No one was coming. They would have to save themselves.

debris =
the remains of something broken or destroyed

Eighteen passengers were killed by the plane's initial crash.

Survivors sat together for warmth in the plane's wreckage.

At first, the passengers had a small amount of food and wine. Although they rationed it carefully, the food was quickly gone. They searched the plane for something else to eat. They found a few snacks, but these quickly ran out. The rocky, icy terrain meant that there were no plants to eat—not even tree bark. The survivors tried to eat anything they could find, from toothpaste to leather from pieces of luggage. But they were still starving. Desperate, the passengers were forced to make an unthinkable decision. They would eat the bodies of the dead to survive.

Sixteen days after the crash, on October 29, the passengers settled down to sleep inside the plane. Suddenly, they heard a terrifying roaring sound. An avalanche came tearing down the mountain. Tons of snow slammed into the plane, burying many of the survivors. Those who still had strength dug desperately to avoid being buried forever in frozen graves. As minutes passed, survivors frantically searched for their friends. An hour later, a second avalanche struck, burying the entire plane. Eight more people died

After the avalanches, days turned into weeks with no sign of rescue. Three men, Roberto Canessa, Nando Parrado, and Antonio Vizintin, volunteered to hike through the mountains to find help. They layered on as much clothing as they could. They also sewed together a three-man sleeping bag from the plane's insulation. They promised the other passengers they would bring back help. After a few days with no sign of help, Parrado and Canessa sent Vizintin back to the plane. They split his remaining supplies between them and pushed ahead.

For days, the two exhausted men walked through the cold. Eventually, the terrain began to change. The snow became lighter, and in some places, it disappeared completely. On the ninth day of their hike, the men found a river. Across it, they spotted a man on horseback. The river's roar was loud, but they heard the rider shout *mañana*—"tomorrow," in Spanish. Parrado and Canessa slept that night near the river. The next day, the rider returned with rescuers. Another rescue team was sent for the remaining passengers on the mountain. After more than two months, sixteen people made it off the mountain alive.

Canessa and Parrado were rescued by mounted police before guiding authorities to the location of their fellow survivors.

10 Tips for Surviving the Cold

1. If possible, build your camp in the woods. Trees can help block the wind.

2. If you don't have a tent, build a shelter such as an igloo or a snow cave.

3. Keep your shelter small to trap body heat inside.

4. Don't build your shelter at the base of a hill or incline. You may be buried by drifting snow or an avalanche.

5. If possible, dig your shelter down into the ground to benefit from the earth's heat.

6. Lay a barrier such as a tarp or pine needles between you and the ground to preserve warmth.

7. Try to build a fire for warmth. The smoke may also help rescuers find you.

8. If you build a fire inside your shelter, make sure there are holes for ventilation.

9. Keep dry to avoid frostbite and hypothermia.

10. Avoid overheating. Sweat can cause you to lose warmth in two ways. When it evaporates, it cools your body. In addition, the moisture from sweat reduces how well clothes insulate you from the cold.

Alone in the Arctic
http://alumweb.mit.edu/classes/1941/Crane.html
This article from *Air Force Magazine* tells more about the incredible survival story of military pilot Leon Crane in Alaska.

Brasch, Nicolas. *Ernest Shackleton's Antarctic Expedition.* New York: PowerKids Press, 2013.
Read this book to learn more about Shackleton's amazing adventure at the bottom of the world.

Cleare, John. *Epic Adventure: Epic Climbs.* New York: Macmillan, 2011.
Meet the pioneers who braved incredible dangers like rock falls, crevasses, whiteouts, and avalanches to summit the world's highest mountains against all odds.

Into the Unknown
http://ngm.nationalgeographic.com/2013/01/mawson-trek/roberts-text
Check out more info and photos from Douglas Mawson's deadly expedition to Antarctica.

Lansing, Alfred. *Endurance: Shackleton's Incredible Voyage.* New York: Basic Books, 2009.
Learn more about Shackleton and his crew in this classic account of the voyage of the *Endurance.* Interviews and diary entries bring the participants to life for modern readers.

Shackleton
http://www.amnh.org/exhibitions/past-exhibitions/shackleton
This museum website has tons of information about Ernest Shackleton's *Endurance* voyage, including maps of the journey.

Woods, Michael, and Mary B. Woods. *Blizzards.* Minneapolis: Lerner Publications Company, 2008.
This book includes firsthand survivor stories—plus the latest facts and figures—to show you blizzards up close.

PHOTO ACKNOWLEDGMENTS

The images in this book are used with the permission of: © iStockphoto/Thinkstock, pp. 4, 8, 15, 16; © cowboy111/Shutterstock Images, p. 5; United States Army Air Forces, p. 6; © Doug Lemke/Shutterstock Images. p. 7; © Bettmann/Corbis/AP Images, p. 9; Frank Hurley, pp. 10, 22; © Mansell/Time & Life Pictures/Getty Images, pp. 11, 21; © prochasson frederic/Shutterstock Images, p. 12; © Classic Vision/age fotostock/SuperStock, p. 13; © IM_photo/Shutterstock Images, p. 14; © Ric Francis/AP Images, p. 17; © Bull's-Eye Arts/Shutterstock Images, p. 18; © Acey Harper/Time & Life Pictures/Getty Images, p. 19; © Topical Press Agency/Hulton Archive/Getty Images, p. 20; © Hulton Archive/Getty Images, p. 23; © kastianz/Shutterstock Images, p. 24; © AP Images, pp. 25, 26, 27; © Max5128/Dreamstime.com, p. 28; © mangojuicy/Shutterstock Images, p. 29.

Front Cover: © Marka/SuperStock.

Main body text set in Calvert MT Std Regular 11/16.
Typeface provided by Monotype Typography.